BASEBALL
Super Stars

By
David Gowdey

Illustrated by
Sam Whitehead

Grosset & Dunlap • New York

AN
MBKA
PRODUCTION

THE SUPER STARS

Superstars bring more than just talent to the game. When a Bonds or a Griffey steps up to the plate or when a Clemens makes his way to the mound, the atmosphere in the ballpark changes. Suddenly there's a charge in the air, and everyone watching can feel it.

Here's an entertaining look at some of baseball's current legends — great athletes who rate with the best ever. Ken Griffey, Jr. and Barry Bonds have already rocketed far beyond their fathers, Ryne Sandberg and Cal Ripken, Jr. perform flawlessly day after day, and Roger Clemens's drive keeps him among the top pitchers every year. Jose Canseco is one of the most exciting players of modern times, and his comeback, whatever its outcome, is one of the top baseball stories of the 1994 season.

Great baseball players do more than rise to the occasion. Great baseball players create the occasion.

BARRY BONDS

Barry Bonds had two favorite players when he was growing up. One was Willie Mays, the legendary San Francisco Giants center fielder; the other was Bobby Bonds, Willie's heir apparent. It's no accident that Barry has always been compared to these two men: Willie Mays is his godfather, and Bobby Bonds is his father.

Barry is understandably sensitive about comparisons. His father had five seasons of 30 home runs and 30 stolen bases, averaging 29 home runs and 40 steals a season over his eleven-year career. Despite Bobby Bonds's power, he often batted leadoff, and son Barry considers him the greatest leadoff hitter ever. Still, he was never able to establish himself as a star in the eyes of the public, bouncing from the Giants to the Yankees, from California to the White Sox, then on to Texas and Cleveland.

Barry was born on July 24, 1964, in Riverside, California. Like Cal Ripken, Jr. and Ken Griffey, Jr. he grew up in major league ballparks. Barry admits with a laugh, however, that he hardly ever watched his father's games: he was too busy calling other kids out of their seats. While his father batted against baseball's best, Barry and his friends played pickup games under the stands using a crumpled paper cup for a ball.

Barry gained more from his father's coaching than from watching him play. Bobby Bonds possessed more speed and power than almost anyone in baseball history. Had he played on a pennant-winning team or led the league in hitting just once, he might have won recognition as one of the all-time greats of the game. As it was, the closest he came was in 1971, his fourth season with the Giants, when his hot hitting carried the team down the stretch to the Western Division title. He ended the season at .288 with 33 homers and 102 RBIs. But in the playoffs Bobby managed only 2 hits in 8 at bats as San Francisco fell in four games to

Roberto Clemente and the Pirates. Outside of the All-Star Game, he never reached the national spotlight again, though as a hitting instructor in Cleveland, Bobby helped develop Joe Carter into one of the game's top power-and-speed threats. His son Barry proved to be just as receptive a pupil.

After high school, Barry entered Arizona State University, where he majored in criminal justice. He won the MVP Award at the NCAA West II Regionals as a freshman and compiled a .347 batting average over his college career. Because of his father's success, Barry says he felt instant pressure when he was drafted sixth overall by the Pittsburgh Pirates in 1985. He reported to the Pirates' Prince William single-A team in the Carolina League and won Player of the Month honors right away, finishing with a .299 average and 13 homers in half a season. The next year he jumped first to triple-A, then up to the majors, joining the Pirates only 44 games into the season.

Barry excelled in football and basketball as well as baseball at Serra High School in San Mateo, California.

acing major league pitching, Barry's verage dipped under .250 for the first me in his life. Still, despite playing only 15 games, he became one of only even rookies in history to hit 15 home uns and steal 30 bases. The next year e hit .261 with 25 homers, and was n his way to stardom.

On December 18, 1989, Barry's wife Susann gave birth to a son, Nikolai Lamar, and Barry's perspective on the world suddenly changed. "When you see how little and helpless he [Nikolai] is, how he depends on you for everything a human being needs to survive, it makes you look at things differently."

Barry is grateful to Pittsburgh manager im Leyland for giving him a chance nd sticking with him when his batting verage was down. "Sometimes failure elps success," he says. "I was one f the players who was allowed to fail, nd I got to understand it, and that nakes success that much better."

Barry hit in the Pirates' leadoff spot rom 1986 to 1989, enjoying solid uccess but never driving in more han 59 runs. Before the 1990 season egan, however, events changed the direction of his career.

During the winter of 1989, Barry engaged in his first prolonged contract negotiations, and was stung by the Pirates' insistence that he'd been a "disappointment." It was a label he couldn't live with. The two sides stayed far apart, and the contract dispute eventually went to arbitration. Barry lost, and the decision cost him more than $800,000 a season.

Up to this time, Barry had had to live with the tag of playing to "less than his potential." Barry knew that his father had lived with it his whole career, and that it had bothered him a great deal.

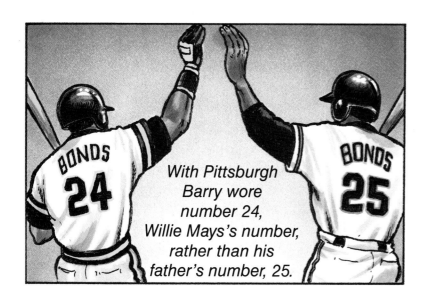

With Pittsburgh Barry wore number 24, Willie Mays's number, rather than his father's number, 25.

Before spring training in 1990, Barry insisted on batting in the fifth spot in the order, where he knew he would get the opportunity to drive in more runs. Manager Leyland mulled it over, then granted him his wish.

Before the season started, Barry's father reminded him that he was capable of hitting for a higher average. After that, Barry became more selective at the plate, and the results were immediate. Batting behind Andy Van Slyke and Bobby Bonilla in the middle of the lineup for the entire 1990 season, he hit 33 home runs, drove in 114 runs, and had a .301 batting average. He also stole 52 bases that year. He became the first player in history to hit 30 home runs, bat .300, drive in 100 runs, score 100 runs, and steal 50 bases in one season.

In 1990, Barry led the National League in slugging percentage (.565) and won the league's Most Valuable Player Award. "All I ever wanted was a chance," he says.

Barry found himself caught up again in prolonged contract negotiations before the 1991 season. His frustration finally erupted in a widely publicized shouting match with manager Leyland in Florida. The argument, caught on video, was soon broadcast all over America. Critics began accusing Barry of putting himself ahead of the team, although Leyland later denied it.

"My mouth — that was probably my greatest regret," Barry says now with a laugh. But at the time, the incident affected him deeply. A month into the 1991 season, he'd hit only 2 home runs and was batting under .200. Barry realized that the Pirates had a strong team and that he might never be that close to a pennant again. Focusing on one at bat at a time, he put up MVP numbers for the rest of the season and finished with 25 home runs and 116 RBIs.

an outstanding catch in foul territory as he ran full speed over a pitching mound in the bullpen. The play could have been dangerous, but Bobby wasn't willing to let up.

The Pirates won the Eastern Division title for the third year in a row, but again, Barry faced his toughest challenge in the league championship series. In previous years he'd been dogged by critics for his subpar playoff performances, and 1992 proved to be no exception. He struggled at the plate as the Atlanta Braves took a 3–1 lead in the series, and was booed by Pittsburgh fans when he struck out with runners on base. It was the first time he'd ever been booed in his home ballpark. "Heck, I understood," he said after the game. "I'd have booed me too."

After the game, Barry visited manager Jim Leyland in the manager's office. Leyland hadn't called him in; Barry simply wanted to talk. He wanted to go over the years he and Leyland had spent together, and maybe find some way to relax in the upcoming game.

In 1992, Barry proved once again that he was a top player in baseball. He won his second straight MVP Award, hitting .311 with 34 home runs, 39 stolen bases, and 103 RBIs, while playing superbly in left field. In the All-Star Game, he made

"I had a tremendous discussion with Barry," said Leyland. "It was almost like a father-son talk. I just said, 'This is the time of life for Barry Bonds. You ought to be the happiest guy in the world. You wait six years for the moment, and when it comes, you don't want it to be negative.'"

After the meeting, Barry was surprised to find ex-Pirate teammate Bobby Bonilla waiting for him. Barry's wife had asked Bonilla to fly in from New York for the next game, and the two friends stayed up all night talking before Barry finally went to sleep at six A.M. Barry had wanted to erase the memory of the bad game, and he knew that sleeping through the day would keep him fresh and give him less time to worry.

The next evening, when he approached the plate for his first at bat, the Pirate fans rose from their seats. Barry drank in the long ovation, then stepped into the batter's box. As the ball streaked in, he locked onto its rotation and sent a ringing double deep to right center field. The crowd roared his name as he stood on second base.

In his next at bat, Barry slashed a single to knock in a run, then stole second base. Late in the game he made a sensational backhand catch to snuff out the Braves' last rally. As he took the field for the ninth inning with the Pirates comfortably ahead, the fans gave him another long standing ovation and Barry waved back.

The game proved to be Pittsburgh's last glimpse of Barry. The Pirates lost the 1992 league championship series to the Braves, and Barry became a free agent. After considering offers from many teams, including the Braves, he surprised everyone by choosing to sign with his father's old team, the San Francisco Giants.

His father's longtime teammate Willie Mays, Barry's godfather, was thrilled when he heard the news. Mays offered to bring his famous number 24 out of retirement. Barry considered it a great honor, but this time he chose to wear his father's number, 25. Within days, the Giants named Dusty Baker, once a Little League teammate of Bobby Bonds, as manager of the club, and Bobby was named batting coach.

In January 1993, as the baseball world was still buzzing over his signing, Barry made a graceful gesture away from the spotlight. He telephoned Giants star Will Clark and assured him that he had no plans to battle Will for the role of the Giants' leader. That role, he insisted, remained Will's.

But in April, it was Barry who led the Giants' charge to the top of the National League West. His torrid hitting raised the confidence level of every player on the team. Matt Williams, hitting in front of Barry, had more home runs by the halfway point than he'd hit in the entire previous season. In a subtle way, Barry's presence affected the pitching, too. Giants pitchers realized that the Giants now had the firepower to come back after falling behind, and they began to challenge hitters much more often. They could throw strikes without having to worry that a single home run ball might cost them the game.

By the All-Star break, Barry was among the top five in nine National League offensive categories. Attendance at Candlestick Park was up and the Giants had baseball's best record. When Barry led all other players in fan balloting for the All-Star Game, it was that rare occasion when everyone in the game — players, owners, fans, and writers — found themselves in complete agreement. Barry Bonds was indeed the best player in baseball.

REGULAR SEASON RECORD

YEAR	TEAM (LEAGUE)	G	AB	R	H	2B	3B	HR	RBI	SB	BB	SO	AVG
1985	Prin. William (Car.)	71	254	49	76	16	4	13	37	15	37	52	.299
1986	Hawaii (Pac. Coast)	44	148	30	46	7	2	7	37	16	33	31	.311
1986	Pittsburgh (NL)	113	413	72	92	26	3	16	48	36	65	102	.223
1987	Pittsburgh (NL)	150	551	99	144	34	9	25	59	32	54	88	.261
1988	Pittsburgh (NL)	144	538	97	152	30	5	24	58	17	72	82	.283
1989	Pittsburgh (NL)	159	580	96	144	34	6	19	58	32	93	93	.248
1990	Pittsburgh (NL)	151	519	104	156	32	3	33	114	52	93	83	.301
1991	Pittsburgh (NL)	153	510	95	149	28	5	25	116	43	107	73	.292
1992	Pittsburgh (NL)	140	473	109	147	36	5	34	103	39	127	69	.311
1993	San Francisco (NL)	159	539	129	181	38	4	46	123	29	126	79	.336
	MAJOR LEAGUE TOTALS	1169	4123	801	1165	258	40	222	679	280	737	669	.283

NATIONAL LEAGUE CHAMPIONSHIP SERIES RECORD

YEAR	TEAM (LEAGUE)	G	AB	R	H	2B	3B	HR	RBI	SB	BB	SO	AVG
1990	Pittsburgh (NL)	6	18	4	3	0	0	0	1	2	6	5	.167
1991	Pittsburgh (NL)	7	27	1	4	1	0	0	0	3	2	4	.148
1992	Pittsburgh (NL)	7	23	5	6	1	0	1	2	1	6	4	.261
	TOTALS	20	68	10	13	2	0	1	3	6	14	13	.191

ALL-STAR GAME RECORD

YEAR	LEAGUE	AB	R	H	2B	3B	HR	RBI	SB	BB	SO	AVG
1990	National	1	0	0	0	0	0	0	0	1	0	.000
1992	National	3	1	1	1	0	0	0	0	0	0	.333
1993	National	3	2	2	2	0	0	0	0	0	0	.667
	TOTALS	7	3	3	3	0	0	0	0	1	0	.429

CAL Ripken Jr.

It was the opening day of the 1982 season, and Baltimore Orioles 21-year-old third baseman Cal Ripken hadn't slept much the night before. In 39 at bats with the team the previous September he'd batted only .128 — 5 hits, all singles. Baltimore manager Earl Weaver had been impressed with the rookie's poise in spring training and made him a starter, but despite his outward confidence a part of Cal still wondered if he was ready for the majors.

Fifty-two thousand fans roared a welcome to the O's as they took the field to battle the Kansas City Royals. The first inning was scoreless, but the Royals scored in the top of the second.

In the bottom of the inning Cal stepped in against Kansas City's ace, Dennis Leonard. He felt the wind at his back and remembered how the ball had carried well in batting practice. Although he'd felt butterflies in his stomach before entering the batter's box, he relaxed as soon as he tapped his bat on the plate. After a winter of waiting, he'd finally reached the place where he felt he belonged. Now he wanted to prove it.

Baltimore's Ken Singleton took a lead off first as Leonard gazed in for the catcher's sign. Cal focused intently on the ball in the pitcher's hand and told himself not to try for the fences. Leonard checked the runner, then pitched — Cal took a strike. On the next pitch Cal swung and met the ball solidly.

The crowd rose to its feet as the ball arched, then settled deep into the left field stands. Cal had given the Orioles the lead with a home run with his first swing of the season, and the roar of approval was deafening.

Cal was so excited that he charged around the bases at close to full speed. Head down, he nearly passed the veteran Singleton on his way to home plate. Looking back years later, Cal called the home run his most memorable moment in baseball.

More challenges were soon on the way. Earl Weaver knew that

Cal had pitched in high school and had an exceptional throwing arm. As a senior he'd gone 7-2 with a 0.70 ERA and 100 strikeouts in 60 innings.

A throw from Cal is virtually without a "loop." It travels across the diamond like a line drive.

Playing a hunch, Weaver switched Cal from third base to shortstop. Weaver knew that Cal's arm strength meant he could play several steps deeper than most shortstops, allowing him to reach ground balls that would otherwise be hits. At 6'5" and 210 pounds Cal became the biggest man ever to play the position regularly in the majors.

Weaver's perceptiveness was soon rewarded. Cal won Rookie of the Year honors in 1982 and the next season the Orioles won the World Series. By 1985 many writers were calling Cal the top player in baseball.

Despite his size, Ripken isn't an overpowering presence on the field. He's comparatively slow on the bases, and rarely hits over .300. Ex-manager Gene Mauch once termed Cal's swing "the worst swing of any great player." Yet Cal is widely regarded as one of the top five shortstops of all time.

Always modest, Cal admits he has talent but insists he's not among the most gifted players in the league. "My advantage is that I know the game well. I grew up in it and had a good teacher in my father."

Cal Ripken, Sr. was a catcher — a taut, lean figure who turned to managing in the minor leagues after his career ended prematurely due to injury. Cal Sr. was often on the road. Cal says, "I learned early that if I wanted to see my father I would have to go to the ballpark with him."

As a boy, Cal Jr. would put on a uniform and shag flies in the outfield. His father told him to be aware of what was going on around him, and when the two drove home together, Cal would be full of questions. "I liked those drives," he smiles.

Cal's mother Vi held the family together during those years, making sure that Cal and his brother Billy arrived at all their Little League games. Very knowledgeable about baseball herself, Vi often gave valuable advice to the boys. The brothers were competitive in many sports, and Cal learned that he had to prepare both physically and mentally beforehand in order to defeat his brother.

Cal Sr. was hired by the Orioles the year Cal Jr. entered high school. At that time the team was built around pitching, power, and great defense. Cal talked to players like Bobby Grich, Al Bumbry, and Don Baylor before games, then bombarded his father with questions afterward. From the beginning, Cal was interested in the subtleties of the game.

Cal says, "The first and last rule of baseball as I was taught it is to catch the ball, then to know what to do with it."

The Orioles' shortstop at the time was Mark Belanger, a light hitter but a truly great fielder. Over the course of the season, Cal came to see that Belanger's defensive play was saving the team dozens of runs, and that even if he didn't hit at all he was worth keeping in the lineup.

Because he knows the opposing hitters so well, Cal's been called a "manager in the infield." He knows he doesn't have the range of most shortstops, so he tries to cut down the area he has to cover: "The way I have success is, I guess, through thinking."

In Cal's rookie season, the Baltimore pitching staff featured four superb starters. Jim Palmer, Dennis Martinez, Mike Flanagan, and Scott McGregor all had fine control, and Cal could count on them to throw each pitch exactly where the catcher signalled. This gave him a great advantage in anticipating where the ball would be hit and then positioning himself to reach it.

Manager Johnny Oates once said, "If I'm pitching and I have runners at first and third with one out in the ninth, the one guy I want the ball hit to is Cal Ripken, because I know the game's over."

When a pitcher has good control, Cal is able to "cheat" and get an extra step or two before the ball reaches him. For example, if Cal sees the pitch is going to be a fastball outside to a right-handed batter, he can cheat towards second base as the pitcher delivers, since the batter isn't likely to pull the ball. When a pitcher isn't as accurate, his fielders are more likely to be caught leaning the wrong way.

A fierce competitor, Cal wants to win at every sport he plays, from wind sprints to Ping-Pong, from basketball to baseball with a taped-up sock in the clubhouse during a rain delay. His attitude rubs off on his teammates. When they see how hard he's working, they push themselves to work harder, too.

Cal's will to win was sorely tested in the summer of 1988, when the Orioles lost 107 games. It was the worst year in team history and one of the worst campaigns of modern times. The Orioles lost their first 21 games in a row. After the first six games, Cal Sr. was fired as manager and Frank Robinson took over the reins — without any better results. Cal slumped during the losing streak, but caught fire in midseason and led all major league shortstops in homers by the end of the year.

The most remarkable feature of Cal's game is his consistency. In fact, he is well on his way to breaking Lou Gehrig's 2,130 consecutive game record which has remained untouched for 53 years.

In May 1925, a 22-year-old from Columbia University named Lou Gehrig came to play for the New York Yankees. For the rest of the 1925 season, Gehrig started every game, hitting .295 with 20 home runs in 437 at bats. He started every game the next season, too, and the next, and the next, and the next. The Iron Horse didn't miss a single game for the next fourteen years — 2,130 consecutive games. He left only after being stricken by the rare disease that would eventually claim his life.

Two years earlier, Cal had one of the greatest seasons in the field any player has ever enjoyed. He made only 3 errors all year, none on grass, and broke the major league record for fewest errors by a shortstop. The Gold Glove that year went to Chicago's Ozzie Guillen, a more spectacular fielder who made 17 errors.

In the summer of 1995, barring injury, Cal Ripken will play his 2,131st game. Cal has now appeared in every game since May 30, 1982 — at one point he played 8,243 consecutive innings.

Some writers feel that if he took an occasional day off his batting average would be higher.

But Cal doesn't think so. After hitting only .250 in 1990 he began to doubt himself, but over the winter he decided that the best cure for doubt is hard work.

"He was on a mission," says pitcher Mike Flanagan. Cal worked out every day in the off-season, and felt more focused when the season started. He was voted again to start the All-Star Game, and in the Home Run Derby held the day before the game, Cal put on a show that will be long remembered. With 22 swings of the bat he hit 12 home runs — his nearest rival hit only 5. "I was probably the most surprised person in the stadium," he said.

Only eight players in the history of baseball have hit 20 home runs in each of their first ten years. Cal is one of them. In 1992 his eleven consecutive seasons of 20 home runs broke Ernie Banks's all-time record for a shortstop.

The next day Cal continued the barrage. He hit a three-run homer, scored the winning run, and was named All-Star MVP. Back in Baltimore, he was presented with the award in a pre-game ceremony and followed up by hitting a homer in that game, too!

He was named American League MVP for the second time at the end of the 1991 season. The next year he was chosen by the fans to start the All-Star Game for a sixth consecutive year, winning more votes than any player in either league since 1982.

Off the field, Cal is still the same low-key, modest person. Asked about his stardom, he deflects the question: ''I want none of that. I've seen what it does to people.''

But manager Johnny Oates sees Cal headed for the Hall of Fame. ''He doesn't do anything that would wake up an opponent. He just beats them,'' says Oates. He ponders a moment, then adds, ''He can be boring to watch for one game. But he's a joy to watch for a season.''

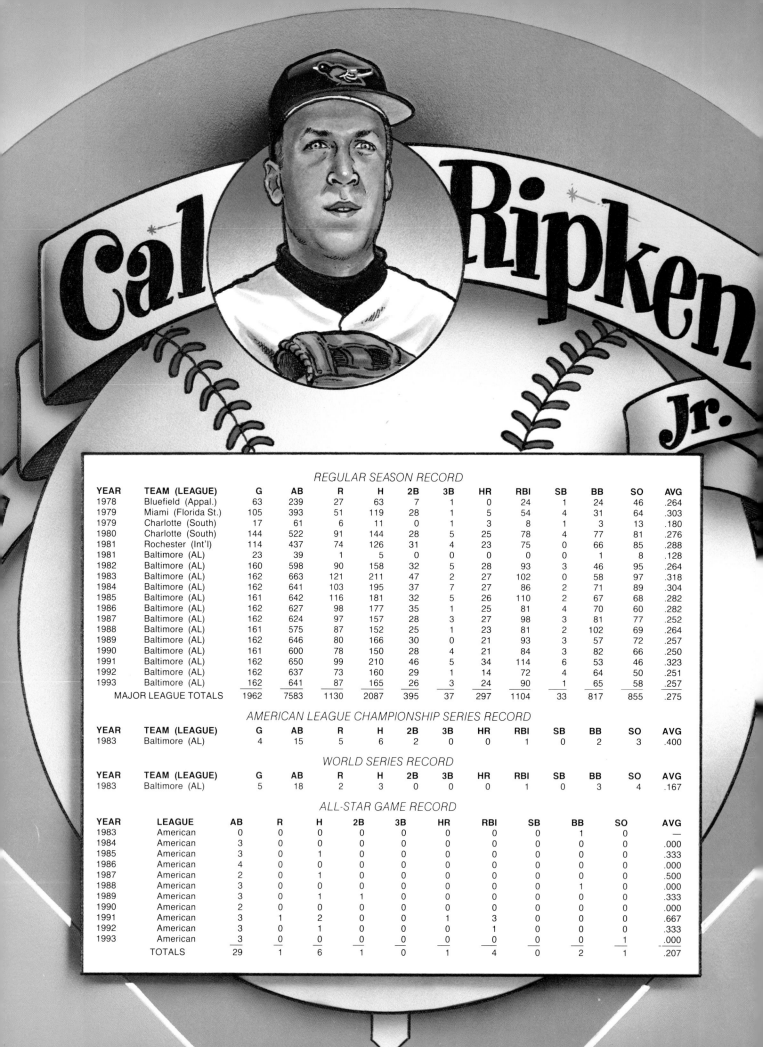

REGULAR SEASON RECORD

YEAR	TEAM (LEAGUE)	G	AB	R	H	2B	3B	HR	RBI	SB	BB	SO	AVG
1978	Bluefield (Appal.)	63	239	27	63	7	1	0	24	1	24	46	.264
1979	Miami (Florida St.)	105	393	51	119	28	1	5	54	4	31	64	.303
1979	Charlotte (South)	17	61	6	11	0	1	3	8	1	3	13	.180
1980	Charlotte (South)	144	522	91	144	28	5	25	78	4	77	81	.276
1981	Rochester (Int'l)	114	437	74	126	31	4	23	75	0	66	85	.288
1981	Baltimore (AL)	23	39	1	5	0	0	0	0	0	1	8	.128
1982	Baltimore (AL)	160	598	90	158	32	5	28	93	3	46	95	.264
1983	Baltimore (AL)	162	663	121	211	47	2	27	102	0	58	97	.318
1984	Baltimore (AL)	162	641	103	195	37	7	27	86	2	71	89	.304
1985	Baltimore (AL)	161	642	116	181	32	5	26	110	2	67	68	.282
1986	Baltimore (AL)	162	627	98	177	35	1	25	81	4	70	60	.282
1987	Baltimore (AL)	162	624	97	157	28	3	27	98	3	81	77	.252
1988	Baltimore (AL)	161	575	87	152	25	1	23	81	2	102	69	.264
1989	Baltimore (AL)	162	646	80	166	30	0	21	93	3	57	72	.257
1990	Baltimore (AL)	161	600	78	150	28	4	21	84	3	82	66	.250
1991	Baltimore (AL)	162	650	99	210	46	5	34	114	6	53	46	.323
1992	Baltimore (AL)	162	637	73	160	29	1	14	72	4	64	50	.251
1993	Baltimore (AL)	162	641	87	165	26	3	24	90	1	65	58	.257
	MAJOR LEAGUE TOTALS	1962	7583	1130	2087	395	37	297	1104	33	817	855	.275

AMERICAN LEAGUE CHAMPIONSHIP SERIES RECORD

YEAR	TEAM (LEAGUE)	G	AB	R	H	2B	3B	HR	RBI	SB	BB	SO	AVG
1983	Baltimore (AL)	4	15	5	6	2	0	0	1	0	2	3	.400

WORLD SERIES RECORD

YEAR	TEAM (LEAGUE)	G	AB	R	H	2B	3B	HR	RBI	SB	BB	SO	AVG
1983	Baltimore (AL)	5	18	2	3	0	0	0	1	0	3	4	.167

ALL-STAR GAME RECORD

YEAR	LEAGUE	AB	R	H	2B	3B	HR	RBI	SB	BB	SO	AVG
1983	American	0	0	0	0	0	0	0	0	1	0	—
1984	American	3	0	0	0	0	0	0	0	0	0	.000
1985	American	3	0	1	0	0	0	0	0	0	0	.333
1986	American	4	0	0	0	0	0	0	0	0	0	.000
1987	American	2	0	1	0	0	0	0	0	0	0	.500
1988	American	3	0	0	0	0	0	0	0	1	0	.000
1989	American	3	0	1	1	0	0	0	0	0	0	.333
1990	American	2	0	0	0	0	0	0	0	0	0	.000
1991	American	3	1	2	0	0	1	3	0	0	0	.667
1992	American	3	0	1	0	0	0	1	0	0	0	.333
1993	American	3	0	0	0	0	0	0	0	0	1	.000
	TOTALS	29	1	6	1	0	1	4	0	2	1	.207

KEN GRIFFEY Jr.

Walk through a schoolyard or a ball field any summer evening and you'll likely see a father playing catch with his son. For over one hundred years baseball has bridged generations, but it's only recently that two generations have appeared in the same major league lineup.

After playing in his first major league game with his son, Ken Sr. remembers "standing in left field and looking over to center, and there's the kid I've played with ever since he was knee-high. This tops my career."

On August 31, 1989, a father and son ran onto the field together as teammates for the first time. Forty-year-old Ken Griffey, Sr. in left field, and 20-year-old Ken Griffey, Jr. in center, warmed up before the first pitch, tossing the ball back and forth like fathers and sons all over the country. Then they settled down to work for the Seattle Mariners.

Ken Sr. later described the first inning as "a dream." Batting second in the bottom of the inning, he stroked a single through the box on the second pitch he saw. Ken Jr., batting third, singled to right on the second pitch to him. Both eventually scored. When they returned to the field for the top of the second, fans rose out of their seats and cheered loud and long.

In the sixth inning the rejuvenated father threw out Bo Jackson as he tried to stretch a single into a double. In the following five games Ken Sr. went 12-for-19, a .632 average, and was named Player of the Week for the first time in his eighteen-year career. "I'm to the point where I wonder what else will happen," he said after winning the honor. He then went out and smacked a three-run homer off Bob Welch to beat the defending champion Oakland A's.

The Mariners won all five of those games following the family reunion. A week later, the two Griffeys blasted back-to-back homers, making more baseball history. "It's about time," joked Ken Sr. as they embraced in the dugout.

There are still plenty of highlights to come for Ken Jr. Hailed as one of the brightest prospects in decades, he keeps improving with every game. At the age of 23, he already has four years of major league playing experience, not to mention a lifetime spent watching his father.

Ken Sr. was drafted by the Cincinnati Reds in 1969. He spent four years in the minor leagues, growing close to his two sons, who were often with him, even on the road. When he finally joined the legendary Big Red Machine, Ken Sr. became a major contributor. The team won world championships in 1975 and 1976.

KEN GRIFFEY

REDS

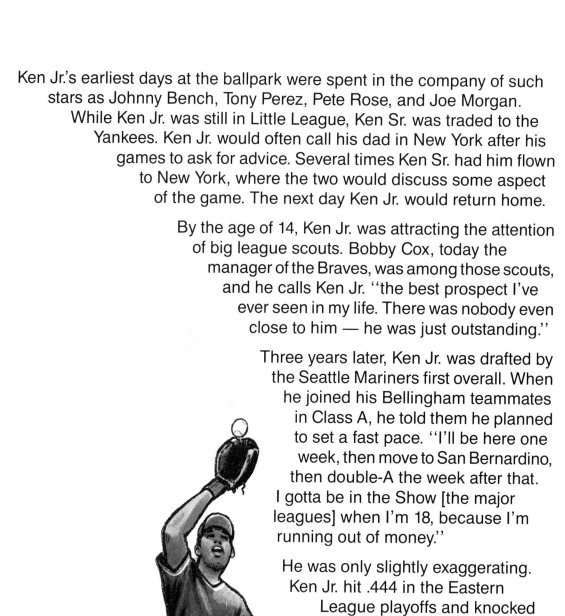

Ken Jr.'s earliest days at the ballpark were spent in the company of such stars as Johnny Bench, Tony Perez, Pete Rose, and Joe Morgan. While Ken Jr. was still in Little League, Ken Sr. was traded to the Yankees. Ken Jr. would often call his dad in New York after his games to ask for advice. Several times Ken Sr. had him flown to New York, where the two would discuss some aspect of the game. The next day Ken Jr. would return home.

By the age of 14, Ken Jr. was attracting the attention of big league scouts. Bobby Cox, today the manager of the Braves, was among those scouts, and he calls Ken Jr. "the best prospect I've ever seen in my life. There was nobody even close to him — he was just outstanding."

Three years later, Ken Jr. was drafted by the Seattle Mariners first overall. When he joined his Bellingham teammates in Class A, he told them he planned to set a fast pace. "I'll be here one week, then move to San Bernardino, then double-A the week after that. I gotta be in the Show [the major leagues] when I'm 18, because I'm running out of money."

He was only slightly exaggerating. Ken Jr. hit .444 in the Eastern League playoffs and knocked in 7 runs in a single game. The next spring he continued at full throttle in the Mariners' camp, hitting .359 and setting team records in hits and RBIs.

SCOUTING REPORT
KEN GRIFFEY JR.

Ken won his spot in the majors while he was still a teenager. When the Mariners' 1989 season began on the road in Oakland, he doubled in his first at bat. And in the Mariners' home opener in Seattle a week later, Ken hit a home run on his first swing in front of the hometown fans.

But his lack of major league experience soon became apparent. Although he grew up around baseball, the younger Griffey's joy always came from playing the game rather than following it. When he entered the American League, he recognized few opposing players' names. He'd never heard of pitchers like Jack Morris or Bob Welch. When a teammate warned him about Bert Blyleven's backdoor curveball, Ken offered his thanks, then asked if Blyleven was a right-hander or a left-hander. Ken's positioning in the outfield was often erratic, too, because he wasn't familiar with the hitters.

Luckily Ken's strong arm and speed in the outfield made up for his inexperience. He finished his first season having assisted in 6 double plays, tops among American League outfielders.

In his first season, Ken made some truly spectacular outfield plays. In one game, he robbed Jesse Barfield of a home run with a brilliant over-the-fence catch at the Seattle Kingdome. In another, he crashed into the Green Monster in Fenway to take a double away from Wade Boggs, then fired a strike from the 375-foot sign in right center field to nail a runner at third base.

When he was 10, Ken Jr. stretched out on a couch and watched his father on TV in the 1980 All-Star Game. That night Ken Sr. was chosen All-Star MVP, and Ken Jr. vowed to himself that one day he would be, too.

Ken Jr. claims to keep no book on opposing pitchers. "I basically go out and have fun," he says. Ken's unwillingness to analyze pitches and hitting may have its own kind of logic. "It just adds more pressure to know what a guy throws," he says. "You start looking for this or that, and all of a sudden he's snuck a 37-mile-per-hour fastball by you."

In 1989, Ken was headed for Rookie of the Year honors, but he broke a bone in his hand in an off-field mishap. When he returned to the team, he made the mistake of trying to do too much at the plate. He had hit 13 home runs by the All-Star break, but added only 3 in the second half of the season.

By the following spring, Ken recovered his poise. His father stressed the importance of waiting for the right pitch, then putting the ball into play. "I've always told him that good things will happen if you're hitting the ball," Ken Sr. says. As a result, Ken Jr.'s strikeout totals remain very low for a young player, despite his carefree attitude.

"I don't know who's pitching tonight," Ken explained before one game. "I couldn't care less. He's still got to throw me something I can hit."

In 1992, voted to start in the All-Star Game himself for the third straight year, Ken Jr. made the most of his chance to follow in his father's MVP footsteps. In the first inning Ken came to bat against Braves pitcher Tom Glavine, who was struggling against the star-filled American League lineup. Ken kept the rally going with a solid single, driving in Mark McGwire for the fourth American League run. In the third inning, facing Greg Maddux, Ken homered deep to left center for another RBI. Then he doubled leading off the sixth, bringing his average in three All-Star Games to a sizzling .652. By the end of the night, Ken had led the American League to a convincing 13–6 win. On that night, Ken Jr. was chosen All-Star MVP.

Ken ended the 1992 season with 103 RBIs, his second straight 100-RBI season, and found himself in some truly elite company. Only five other players have ever driven in 100 runs in back-to-back seasons before the age of 23: Al Kaline, Ty Cobb, Mel Ott, Ted Williams, and Joe DiMaggio. Ken's manager in the 1992 All-Star Game, Tom Kelly, might have put it best when he said after the game, ''He doesn't have a ceiling I can see.''

REGULAR SEASON RECORD

YEAR	TEAM (LEAGUE)	G	AB	R	H	2B	3B	HR	RBI	SB	BB	SO	AVG
1987	Belling. (N'west)	54	182	43	57	9	1	14	40	13	44	42	.313
1988	San Bern. (Calif.)	58	219	50	74	13	3	11	42	32	34	39	.338
1988	Vermont (Eastern)	17	61	10	17	5	1	2	10	4	5	12	.279
1989	Seattle (AL)	127	455	61	120	23	0	16	61	16	44	83	.264
1990	Seattle (AL)	155	597	91	179	28	7	22	80	16	63	81	.300
1991	Seattle (AL)	154	548	76	179	42	1	22	100	18	71	82	.327
1992	Seattle (AL)	142	565	83	174	39	4	27	103	10	44	67	.308
1993	Seattle (AL)	156	582	113	180	38	3	45	109	17	96	91	.309
MAJOR LEAGUE TOTALS		734	2747	424	832	170	15	132	453	77	318	404	.303

ALL-STAR GAME RECORD

YEAR	LEAGUE	AB	R	H	2B	3B	HR	RBI	SB	BB	SO	AVG
1990	American	2	0	0	0	0	0	0	0	1	0	.000
1991	American	3	0	2	0	0	0	0	0	0	0	.667
1992	American	3	2	3	1	0	1	2	0	0	0	1.000
1993	American	3	1	1	0	0	0	1	0	0	1	.333
TOTALS		11	3	6	1	0	1	3	0	1	1	.545

JOSE Canseco

Three weeks into the 1988 season, a small group of reporters heard Jose Canseco make a startling prediction. They'd been discussing how hard it was to make the 30-30 club — to hit 30 home runs and steal 30 bases in the same season. Only a handful of players had ever accomplished the feat. Canseco stretched, and in his careless, offhand style, stated simply, ''I'm going to go 40-40 this year. I'm going to go for it. Because I do have the ability to do it.'' Canseco's pronouncement might have been easily forgotten, except for the fact that he was right. He hit 42 home runs and stole 40 bases that season, becoming the first 40-40 player in major league history. And in the words of Hall of Fame pitcher Dizzy Dean, ''It ain't braggin' if you can do it.''

Jose played third base in his senior year in high school, with brother Ozzie pitching.

Jose Canseco thrives on the publicity and extra pressure that such bold statements bring. But at the same time he seems remote and intensely private. Few people around him can say that they really know him. He can be friendly and boyish one moment, arrogant and aloof the next. He's worked hard to maintain a powerful physique, yet he's often accused of "dogging it" in the outfield. "I think a lot of people misunderstand me," he says. Jose has gone his own way almost all of his life, and if that hasn't always made him popular, it has made him the most dynamic and colorful baseball figure of recent years.

Jose was born in Havana, Cuba, on July 2, 1964, one of identical twins. His parents immigrated to Miami before he and his brother Ozzie were a year old. Jose played baseball in high school, but he wasn't considered a star until his senior year. He was cut from the varsity team in his first two tries, and can't even be found in his high school yearbook, having missed picture day.

Oakland A's scout Camilo Pascual soon noticed something about the big third baseman that no one else had seen. Pascual had been a first-rate pitcher with the Washington Senators and the Minnesota Twins in the 1960s. He could see that Canseco's bat speed was tremendous, major league caliber, and he knew that it would be very tough for a pitcher to get a ball past him if Jose became more selective at the plate.

Canseco hit .400 as a senior, but he was ignored by the major league scouting bureau. When Oakland management met to prepare draft-day strategy, however, Pascual insisted on drafting Jose. When they still seemed dubious, Pascual began to pull bills out of his own pockets, insisting, ''I like him so much, I'll give him my own money.''

In 1982, Jose signed with the A's and his brother Ozzie signed with the Yankees. While both played in the low minors for two years, their father had a standing offer to them: five dollars for each home run hit. The practice became expensive when his sons' careers took off. Still, in 1984 he only had to pay Jose fifteen times. Jose admits that he was still learning about himself and what he was capable of doing.

Also that year, Jose's mother died unexpectedly. The event profoundly changed his life. ''I guess I opened my eyes,'' he says. ''I realized baseball wasn't everything in life.

''At the minor level you take baseball so seriously. When you fail you tend to take it out on yourself too much, and all that does is hurt you. You become frustrated and don't concentrate.

''I decided if it became clear one day I wasn't going to be successful, I would just let it go. From then, I got better and better.''

In 1985, Canseco tore through the minors, making the jump from double-A to the major leagues in one season. With double-A Huntsville he hit .318 with 25 homers and 80 RBIs in just 58 games; he added 11 more homers in Tacoma in 60 games at triple-A, then 5 more in 29 games for the A's, for a total of 41 home runs and 140 RBIs on three different levels in a single season.

On September 22, 1985, Jose Canseco joined a select group of players by hitting a ball over the left field roof of Comiskey Park in Chicago.

BOOM!

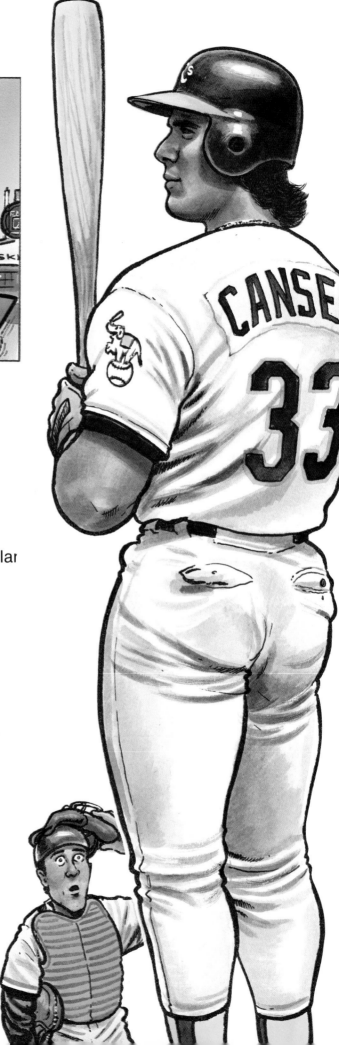

In his first full major league season, Jose turned heads everywhere he played. His physique was startling on a baseball field — his muscular neck and arms bulged dramatically out of his jersey. Although he was 6'4" and 240 pounds, he was neither the tallest nor the heaviest player in baseball. But he seemed like the biggest man on the field wherever he played.

When Jose gripped the bat and whipped it around, it would appear to bend in the air before meeting the ball. Batting practices turned into home run derbies as Jose hit gargantuan drives out of every ballpark, and he usually carried the fireworks over into the game.

Canseco hit 33 homers and drove in 117 runs his first full season, but his batting average slipped to .240 and his play in the outfield was inadequate. He worked hard to improve both over the next season. By 1988 he'd become the hottest player in baseball. His 42 home runs, 40 steals, and 124 RBIs won him MVP honors and propelled the A's to the American League pennant.

Jose has remarkable concentration at the plate. The "zone" he enters has no place for anything outside of the pitcher and the baseball. "You don't even hear the fans, you're so locked in," he says. When his concentration is at its best, "it looks like the ball is suspended in air."

Jose and A's first baseman Mark McGwire began the practice of bumping each other's forearms after a home run instead of shaking hands. The two ''Bash Brothers'' accounted for 74 home runs and 223 RBIs in 1988 and led the A's to a four-game sweep of the San Francisco Giants in the 1989 World Series.

The next spring Jose predicted he would go 50-50 that season; but it was not to be. Several controversial off-field incidents and arrests and various ailments brought him back down to earth, and he appeared in only 65 games. But he won more believers in game four of the American League Championship Series against Toronto by hitting one of the longest home runs in baseball history. In the third inning, with Oakland leading in the series two games to one, Canseco hit a titanic shot to give the A's a commanding lead. Many observers felt that Jose's home run instantly deflated the Toronto Blue Jays' confidence and played a large part in the A's five-game series victory.

Jose swings with fantastic speed, but his muscles look completely relaxed. His fluid swing lets him move with the pitch.

In 1990, Jose hit 37 homers with 101 RBIs, and in 1991, he led the American League with 44 home runs. Still, controversy shadowed his personal life. The A's continued to accept his explanations, but it was obvious that the front office's patience was growing thin.

In recent years, Jose's reputation has prompted fans in many cities to give him a rough ride. He has accepted it with good humor, however, and even with all the distractions he has remained a powerful force on the field.

Early in 1992, he led the A's to a dramatic comeback victory over the New York Yankees with a late-inning grand slam. By mid-August the A's were in first place, seven games ahead of the Minnesota Twins. It looked like another appearance for Jose in the World Series, but in a game in late August, as he was kneeling in the on-deck circle waiting to bat, manager Tony LaRussa tapped him on the shoulder and called him back to the dugout. He'd been traded to the Texas Rangers in exchange for three players.

BONK!

Like every fan in the Bay Area, Jose was shocked. "Maybe I'd worn out my welcome there," he said with a shrug. But he refused to let it bother him. Besides, he'd always claimed that the spacious Oakland Coliseum took home runs away. In fact, just after he'd made his 40-40 prediction in 1988 he added, "If I was playing in any other ballpark, say Texas, 40-40 would be an every year event."

Jose fell short of the mark in his first year with the Rangers. Pleased to be in the same lineup as defending home run champion Juan Gonzalez, he began the season strongly and was among the American League's leaders in RBIs. Canseco and Gonzalez drove to the park together every day, and the two friends presented a fearsome challenge for American League pitchers.

In June, during a one-sided game against Boston, manager Kevin

Kennedy kept an earlier promise and allowed Jose a chance to pitch. Although Jose felt a twinge in his elbow when he warmed up in the bullpen, he took the mound. On his second pitch he tore ligaments, but he continued to throw, aggravating the damage. Surgery was performed on July 9, and Jose was finished for the year. He was upset, but he soon vowed to return to the Rangers stronger than ever.

His comeback is sure to generate plenty of interest. Jose still considers himself first an "entertainer," and he often goes out on a limb with his predictions. He's attracted many critics, but he's willing to answer their questions. Being the center of attention has never fazed him. "That's where there's no room for failure," he says. "That's where you have to produce. That's where the real excitement is."

REGULAR SEASON RECORD

YEAR	TEAM (LEAGUE)	G	AB	R	H	2B	3B	HR	RBI	SB	BB	SO	AVG
1982	Miami (Florida St.)	6	9	0	1	0	0	0	0	0	1	3	.111
1982	Idaho Falls (Pio.)	28	57	13	15	3	0	2	7	3	9	13	.263
1983	Madison (Midwest)	34	88	8	14	4	0	3	10	2	10	36	.159
1983	Medford (N'west)	59	197	34	53	15	2	11	40	6	30	78	.269
1984	Modesto (Calif.)	116	410	61	113	21	2	15	73	10	74	127	.276
1985	Huntsville (South)	58	211	47	67	10	2	25	80	6	30	55	.318
1985	Tacoma (PCL)	60	233	41	81	16	1	11	47	5	40	66	.348
1985	Oakland (AL)	29	96	16	29	3	0	5	13	1	4	31	.302
1986	Oakland (AL)	157	600	85	144	29	1	33	117	15	65	175	.240
1987	Oakland (AL)	159	630	81	162	35	3	31	113	15	50	157	.257
1988	Oakland (AL)	158	610	120	187	34	0	42	124	40	78	128	.307
1989	Huntsville (South)	9	29	2	6	0	0	0	3	1	5	11	.207
1989	Oakland (AL)	65	227	40	61	9	1	17	57	6	23	69	.269
1990	Oakland (AL)	131	481	83	132	14	2	37	101	19	72	158	.274
1991	Oakland (AL)	154	572	115	152	32	1	44	122	26	78	152	.266
1992	Oak.-Texas (AL)	119	439	74	107	15	0	26	87	6	63	128	.244
1993	Texas (AL)	60	231	30	59	14	1	10	46	6	16	62	.255
	MAJOR LEAGUE TOTALS	1032	3886	644	1033	185	9	245	780	134	449	1060	.266

AMERICAN LEAGUE CHAMPIONSHIP SERIES RECORD

YEAR	TEAM (LEAGUE)	G	AB	R	H	2B	3B	HR	RBI	SB	BB	SO	AVG
1988	Oakland (AL)	4	16	4	5	1	0	3	4	1	1	2	.313
1989	Oakland (AL)	5	17	1	5	0	0	1	3	0	3	7	.294
1990	Oakland (AL)	4	11	3	2	0	0	0	1	2	5	5	.182
	TOTALS	13	44	8	12	1	0	4	8	3	9	14	.273

WORLD SERIES RECORD

YEAR	TEAM (LEAGUE)	G	AB	R	H	2B	3B	HR	RBI	SB	BB	SO	AVG
1988	Oakland (AL)	5	19	1	1	0	0	1	5	1	2	4	.053
1989	Oakland (AL)	4	14	5	5	0	0	1	3	1	4	3	.357
1990	Oakland (AL)	4	12	1	1	0	0	1	2	0	2	3	.083
	TOTALS	13	45	7	7	0	0	3	10	2	8	10	.156

ALL-STAR GAME RECORD

YEAR	LEAGUE	AB	R	H	2B	3B	HR	RBI	SB	BB	SO	AVG
1986	American				Did not play							
1988	American	4	0	0	0	0	0	0	0	0	1	.000
1989	American				Did not play							
1990	American	4	0	0	0	0	0	0	0	1	1	1	.000
1992	American				Did not play							
	TOTALS	8	0	0	0	0	0	0	0	1	1	2	.000

ROGER CLEMENS

On the night of April 28, 1986, Boston Red Sox pitcher Roger Clemens made a place for himself in the record books. After a sluggish spring training, he'd been pitching well in the early season. That night he felt strong. The Seattle Mariners and 13,414 Fenway Park fans would soon realize just how strong.

The next morning, baseball fans all over the country gaped in disbelief when they read the box score of the game:

	IP	R	ER	H	W	K
Clemens WP (4–0)	9	1	1	3	0	20

Roger had fanned the side in the first, fourth, and fifth innings — he had 12 strikeouts after five innings and 16 after seven. His control was remarkable — after the sixth inning he didn't go to 3 balls on a single batter. Mariner Gorman Thomas's solo home run in the seventh finally broke the scoreless tie, and Clemens blew up after the inning, trashing part of the Red Sox dugout. Then the Sox answered with Dwight Evans's three-run homer in the bottom of the inning, and the game was all but over.

"Late in the game I knew something was happening," said Roger afterward. "All the fans were behind me."

Red Sox pitching coach Bill Fischer said after the game, "I almost had tears in my eyes. It was the best game I ever saw pitched." Of Roger's 138 pitches,

97 were strikes — and there were no argued calls all night. Catcher Rich Gedman described the Mariner hitters when they stepped in to face Clemens like this: "They looked like they wanted to say something, but just didn't know what to say."

The game had a significant impact on the pennant race. The Red Sox had gone into the game with a 9–8 record, three games out of first place, but Clemens's super effort ignited them. They tore off 12 wins in their next 14 games and charged into first place.

By July, Roger was 12–0 and the Red Sox were eight games up. They would go on to win the division title and the American League pennant. Roger cruised to a 24–4 record, won A.L. MVP honors, and was a unanimous choice for the Cy Young Award. In fact, since that night in late April 1986, Roger Clemens has been regarded as the dominant pitcher in baseball.

Roger Clemens was born in Dayton, Ohio, on August 4, 1962. He never knew his father — his mother Bess moved away from him when Roger was eight weeks old. Roger, his two older brothers, and his younger sister were raised by their mother and her second husband, a truck driver named Woody Booher, first in Tennessee and then in Texas.

Woody died when Roger was nine years old, but Roger remembers him well. He was a big, stern man, a powerful father figure who, in Roger's words, "kept order real easy."

After Woody's death Roger grew closer to his family, particularly his brothers Richard and Randy and his grandmother Myrtle Lee, or "Mammy." His mother and Mammy made certain that he didn't let the hard times affect him too much. As a result, Roger developed a tremendous inner discipline and a drive to succeed that has never left him.

Even in his rookie season, nervousness on the mound was never a problem for Roger. In his first year the on-base percentage of the first man each inning was a paltry .239 — he struck out 32 leadoff batters while walking only 3.

... COOL AND STEADY!

At age 22, Roger seemed well on his way to a great career. But his iron will soon began to work against him. In Roger's second season, his drive and ambition came close to destroying him before he had even begun.

Roger attended the University of Texas, and was part of the famous Texas pitching program that has developed such major leaguers as Greg Swindell and Bobby Witt. He was young and strong, and never wanted to be taken out of a game. Like many other college pitchers, he threw a lot of innings over a short period of time.

After going 9–4 in his rookie season in the majors, Roger cruised through the summer of 1985 growing more confident with every game. He felt twinges in his arm and sometimes sharp pain, but even throwing at 80 percent of normal strength, Roger was blowing batters away.

When the Red Sox dropped out of the pennant race in 1985, they placed Roger on the disabled list and told him to rest his arm. Roger tried, but he was young and impatient. He wanted to get back as soon as he could, and he wanted to be as strong as possible. So Roger continued to work out in secret, going from lifting weights to tossing a ball to full-scale pitching off a mound.

The results were disastrous. Roger's shoulder began to throb, even when he wasn't throwing. Clearly something had to be done. In a rare operation, the famous sports surgeon Dr. Frank Jobe cut muscles that stretched between his arm and shoulder — the muscles had been so tight and overdeveloped that they'd put a strain on his arm when he threw.

After the operation, Roger continued a weight routine for his legs but agreed not to put stress on his upper body at all. He entered training camp the next season not knowing if he'd be on the opening day roster. His early outings that spring were short, but he made rapid progress. By opening day, Roger was ready to contribute.

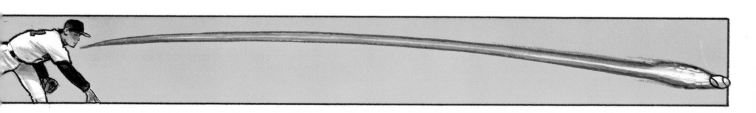

PONG!

Different explanations for the source of Roger's talent have been offered. Some people believe that his stamina is related to his walking three miles to school each day, flinging rocks at targets along the way. Others point to his willingness to keep working until he'd mastered not just the fastball and curve, but a sinking fastball, slider, and forkball, as well. It may be that the competitive drive instilled in him by his mother and grandmother played the biggest part. At 92, Mammy still manages to get out to the park to watch her grandson pitch.

Roger has put a great deal of effort into learning the physics of pitching. By studying with personal trainers like film star Chuck Norris, he's learned which muscles need to be developed. All his teammates agree that he's the hardest worker on the team. And his hard work has served him well — he has the endurance to throw over 140 pitches a game if he has to.

One of Roger's favorite exercises is dipping his arm over and over into a barrel of raw rice kernels, digging his fingers as deep as he can.

RICE

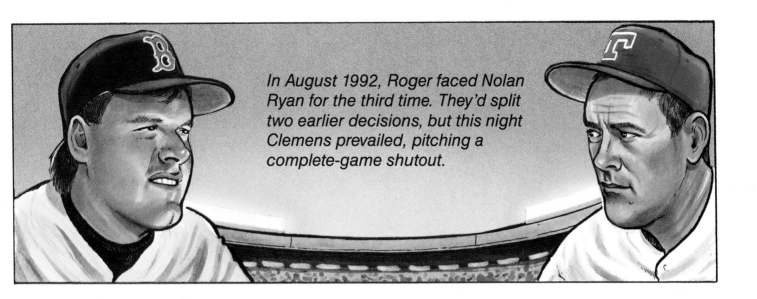

In August 1992, Roger faced Nolan Ryan for the third time. They'd split two earlier decisions, but this night Clemens prevailed, pitching a complete-game shutout.

Roger knows that Tom Seaver and Nolan Ryan, the pitchers he most looked up to as a boy, were able to develop their pitching by developing tremendous strength in their legs and hips. Roger's pitching motion is a blend of the motions of his two favorite pitchers, with an emphasis on leg drive and follow-through.

Year in and year out, Roger Clemens has been among baseball's elite players. Several pitchers have approached his accomplishments in a single year's performance. Orel Hershiser, for example, broke Don Drysdale's 20-year-old record by pitching 59 scoreless innings in 1988. But no pitcher has come close to matching Clemens's greatest strength — his consistency.

Roger's cap, shoes, and glove from his 20-strikeout game are prominently displayed today in the Baseball Hall of Fame, and there is little doubt that Clemens himself will be enshrined there soon after his career is over.

Between 1986 and 1992, Roger won more games than any other player, posting an ERA over 3.00 only once, winning over 60 percent of his decisions, and striking out over 200 batters each year — the only player in major league history to do so. He won the Cy Young Award as the league's top pitcher in 1986, 1987, and 1991.

Today Tony Peña, Roger's current catcher with the Red Sox, sometimes gets so carried away when the pitcher is in a groove that he stops calling signals. When the ball blazes over the plate at 98 miles per hour, Tony simply waves his glove for more of the same, and on occasion has even told batters, ''Here comes the fastball!'' It never makes any difference. No one can touch Roger when he's at his best.

ROGER CLEMENS

REGULAR SEASON RECORD

YEAR	TEAM (LEAGUE)	W	L	ERA	G	CG	IP	H	R	ER	SO	BB	ShO
1983	Winter Haven (FSL)	3	1	1.24	4	3	29	22	4	4	36	0	1
1983	New Britain (East)	4	1	1.38	7	1	52	31	8	8	59	12	1
1984	Pawtucket (Int'l)	2	3	1.93	7	3	46²/₃	39	12	10	50	14	1
1984	Boston (AL)	9	4	4.32	21	5	133¹/₃	146	67	64	126	29	1
1985	Boston (AL)	7	5	3.29	15	3	98¹/₃	83	38	36	74	37	1
1986	Boston (AL)	24	4	2.48	33	10	254	179	77	70	238	67	1
1987	Boston (AL)	20	9	2.97	36	18	281²/₃	248	100	93	256	83	7
1988	Boston (AL)	18	12	2.93	35	14	264	217	93	86	291	62	8
1989	Boston (AL)	17	11	3.13	35	8	253¹/₃	215	101	88	230	93	3
1990	Boston (AL)	21	6	1.93	31	7	228¹/₃	193	59	49	209	54	4
1991	Boston (AL)	18	10	2.62	35	13	271¹/₃	219	93	79	241	65	4
1992	Boston (AL)	18	11	2.41	32	11	246²/₃	203	80	66	208	62	5
1993	Boston (AL)	11	14	4.46	29	2	191²/₃	175	99	95	160	67	1
	MAJOR LEAGUE TOTALS	163	86	2.94	302	91	2222²/₃	1878	807	726	2033	619	35

AMERICAN LEAGUE CHAMPIONSHIP SERIES RECORD

YEAR	TEAM (LEAGUE)	W	L	ERA	G	CG	IP	H	R	ER	SO	BB	ShO
1986	Boston (AL)	1	1	4.37	3	0	22²/₃	22	12	11	17	7	0
1988	Boston (AL)	0	0	3.86	1	0	7	6	3	3	8	0	0
1990	Boston (AL)	0	1	3.52	2	0	7²/₃	7	3	3	4	5	0
	TOTALS	1	2	4.10	6	0	37¹/₃	35	18	17	29	12	0

WORLD SERIES RECORD

YEAR	TEAM (LEAGUE)	W	L	ERA	G	CG	IP	H	R	ER	SO	BB	ShO
1986	Boston (AL)	0	0	3.18	2	0	11¹/₃	9	5	4	11	6	0

ALL-STAR GAME RECORD

YEAR	LEAGUE	W	L	ERA	CG	IP	H	R	ER	SO	BB	ShO
1986	American	1	0	0.00	0	3	0	0	0	2	0	0
1988	American	0	0	0.00	0	1	0	0	0	1	0	0
1990	American				Did not play							
1991	American	0	0	9.00	0	1	1	1	1	0	0	0
1992	American	0	0	0.00	0	1	2	0	0	0	0	0
	TOTALS	1	0	1.50	0	6	3	1	1	3	0	0

RYNE SANDBERG

Over the last decade, Ryne Sandberg has firmly established himself among the greatest baseball players ever. He hits for average and power, gets on base a high percentage of the time, has stolen over 300 bases, and has won the Gold Glove Award as the National League's best-fielding second baseman more often than anyone in the Baseball Hall of Fame. Top baseball analyst Bill James ranks Sandberg as one of the four best second basemen ever — along with Joe Morgan, Eddie Collins, and Rogers Hornsby — and compares him to Willie Mays as the closest thing he's ever seen to a perfect player.

Playing for the Chicago Cubs, one of America's favorite and most visible teams, would seem to ensure Sandberg a permanent place in the national spotlight. But Ryne's self-effacing manner often deflects the media, and he doesn't attract as much attention as many lesser players do. After a game, Ryne's more likely to remark upon a teammate's play than to talk about himself.

A fearless, agile runner with a very strong arm, Ryne was voted all-state quarterback in high school.

Ryne Dee Sandberg was born in Spokane, Washington, on September 18, 1959. His parents named him after a popular New York Yankee of the time, fireballing relief pitcher Ryne Duren. In school, Ryne competed in sports all year round and earned all-city honors in both baseball and basketball. But it was in football, as a quarterback for North Central High School, that his talents really stood out.

Recruited by such college football powers as UCLA, USC, Oklahoma, and Nebraska, Ryne nearly accepted a scholarship to Nebraska. But he finally decided to stay close to home, and in the spring of 1978 signed a letter of intent with Washington State. Then in June, just after graduating from high school, he was drafted as a baseball player by the Philadelphia Phillies. Although he wasn't picked until the twentieth round, the Phillies offered him a substantial signing bonus.

Ryne weighed his choices carefully. He knew that if he failed in pro baseball he could always return to school. He visited several different colleges, walked around the campuses, and took a look at the football teams. When he saw the size of the linemen he'd be playing against, his dreams of an NFL career were jolted. He said later that he never regretted deciding to play baseball: ''How could I be a professional quarterback if I got killed playing in college?''

Ryne progressed rapidly through the minors. He led the Pioneer League in assists and double plays his first season, and after a year in single-A ball was selected to the double-A Eastern League All-Star team in 1980. Playing shortstop for the Phillies' Oklahoma City farm club, he hit .293 in 1981 and was called up to the parent club in September.

Ryne was a raw talent when he first arrived in Philadelphia. He was fast and a good fielder, but the Phillies didn't feel he was polished enough to start at shortstop in the major leagues. And when they looked for other places to play him, they found an established player in every position. All-time great Mike Schmidt was set at third base, brilliant fielder Manny Trillo held down second, and Garry Maddox was a proven star in center field. In addition, talented players like Julio Franco and Juan Samuel were in the minors on the verge of breaking in. That September, Ryne batted only six times.

Ryne signed with the Phillies in the summer of 1978 and began a pro baseball career. Ironically, this meant that his earlier decision to stay close to home was completely undone — over the next three years he played for towns in Montana, South Carolina, Pennsylvania, and Oklahoma.

During the winter of 1981–82, the Phillies began to pursue Ivan DeJesus, the Cubs shortstop who was several years younger than their current starter, Larry Bowa. Phillies chief scout Hugh Alexander offered a straight swap, Bowa for DeJesus, but Cubs general manager Dallas Green held out for more.

Green had just moved to the Cubs after building the Phillies into a World Series champion. He knew Sandberg had potential, and he knew the Phillies had plenty of other young talent. He insisted Ryne be included, and Alexander finally agreed. Today, when asked why he made the trade, Alexander simply shakes his head. "If I knew he was going to be this good," he says ruefully, "do you think I would've traded him?"

Ryne's first years in Chicago were mostly unmemorable. He started for the club at

third base, but hit only 7 home runs and 54 RBIs — hardly the kind of power statistics expected from a major league third baseman.

His fielding remained steady, and after acquiring veteran third baseman Ron Cey, the Cubs decided to try Ryne at second.

Hugh Alexander points out that the second baseman has a tougher job on the double play than the shortstop: "The second baseman can't be scared. A shortstop is coming across the bag and looking at the runner coming at him, but the second baseman is at the runner's mercy." Alexander praises Ryne highly, comparing him to the great Bill Mazeroski: "He can jump away from that runner at the last second. He hangs in there, but you don't get to him."

Ryne's years as a football player helped make him fearless on the pivot at second base when

opposing runners barrel in to try to break up the double play.

Ryne continued to improve as a hitter, but it wasn't until Jim Frey came in as general manager in 1984 that the young star came into his own. Frey told Ryne that he'd be able to hit for more power if he became more aggressive at the plate. Instead of trying to win a race to first whenever he hit the ball, Frey suggested,

"Wouldn't it be a nice feeling to jog around the bases?" Ryne was surprised, but he succeeded in changing his style. In 1984, he began trying to pull the ball to left field.

The results were dramatic. Ryne hit 19 homers and 36 doubles, led the league with 19 triples, and drove in 84 runs. The Cubs, who'd finished with a 71–91 record the year before, pushed all the way to a division title.

Ryne's speed was his greatest asset early in his career, and he set a Chicago record for third basemen by stealing 32 bases in his rookie year.

Many observers point to the Saturday afternoon of June 23, 1984, as the key date of the season. The Cubs' battle that day against the first-place St. Louis Cardinals was also a major turning point in Ryne's career.

After the Cubs gave up a run in the top of the first, Ryne's single in the bottom of the inning drove in a run to tie the score. St. Louis chased Cubs starter Steve Trout with 6 runs in the second and led 7–1 going into the fifth. Ryne knocked in another run in the bottom of the inning, but the Cardinals came back with two more in the top of the sixth.

It's a well-known fact in the bleachers that no lead is safe at Wrigley Field if the wind is blowing out. In the bottom of the sixth the Cubs rallied again, and Ryne's two-run single off Neil Allen tightened the score to 9–8.

Ryne batted again leading off the top of the ninth. With the score still 9–8, the Cardinals sent out their ace stopper, Bruce Sutter, to try to nail down the win. But Ryne had other ideas. He jumped on Sutter's split-fingered fastball and hit a long home run to tie the game and send it into extra innings.

But Ryne still wasn't through. The Cardinals scored twice in the top of the tenth, but with two out in the bottom of the inning, Cubs leadoff man Bob Dernier walked, and Ryne faced Sutter again. Again he connected, and the ball carried deep into the center field seats.

The Cubs went on to win the game in the bottom of the eleventh, beginning a winning streak that would carry them to an Eastern Division title. Looking back on the game, Ryne admits, "We kind of amazed ourselves that day." Ryne had gone 5-for-6 with 7 RBIs and had tied the game with a home run twice in two innings. After the game, Cardinals manager Whitey Herzog, who'd faced such stars as Mickey Mantle and Roberto Clemente during his long career, called Ryne "the best baseball player I've ever seen."

Ryne won the MVP Award at the end of the 1984 season and has finished near the top in balloting every year since. In 1985, he became just the third player in history to hit 25 home runs while stealing 50 bases. And he once went an entire season without making a single throwing error.

In 1986, Ryne set an all-time fielding record, making just 5 errors in 806 chances. Three years later he set a single season record for second basemen by going 89 straight games without making an error.

In 1990, "Ryno" hit 40 home runs and became the first second baseman since Rogers Hornsby in 1925 to lead the National League in that category. And he's the only second baseman ever to hit 30 homers and steal 20 bases in the same season.

A model of consistency, Ryne never allows himself to get too high on a good night or too low on a bad one. "He's the same guy," remarks friend Doug Dascenzo. "You can't tell the difference. He's quiet. He doesn't complain. He just does his job." And it's an attitude that has kept public attention focused on other, less predictable players.

Many sportswriters try to manufacture feuds between players and management, or players and other players, but controversy just isn't Ryne's style. He's a throwback to the days when a baseball player did most of his talking through his actions on the field. Ryne once remarked that if he's in a room with someone else and that person doesn't say anything, then there won't be a conversation. Older fans remember Joe DiMaggio's attitude as much the same. DiMaggio and his Yankee teammates used to sit in their hotel lobby for hours on end without speaking or reading, just sitting, watching the other guests come and go. Sandberg isn't quite as austere, but he remains intensely private.

Although writers have a hard time squeezing original quotes out of him, Ryne is often sought out by younger teammates for advice. And he's a team leader off the field, too. In 1990, he pledged $100 for every home run, triple, double, single, stolen base, RBI, and run scored, then proceeded to have his finest offensive season ever. Altogether, his numbers added up to a donation of over $42,000.

When he's not playing, Ryne spends most of his time with his family, and stays away from card conventions and commercial endorsements. Occasionally his wry sense of humor surfaces. On hearing that he'd been named one of *People* magazine's "50 Most Beautiful People," Sandberg said in his low-key way, "I didn't think I belonged in the Top 50 — Top 55, yes, but not the Top 50." He denies that he's reached his peak. "I'm just trying to become a complete player," he once told a reporter, adding with a grin, "Bet you've never heard that one before."

Only rarely do the fans in the Wrigley Field bleachers reach a consensus, but on one point there's virtual unanimity: If there's anyone in baseball who's earned the label of "complete player," it's Ryne Sandberg.

Ryne Sandberg

REGULAR SEASON RECORD

YEAR	TEAM (LEAGUE)	G	AB	R	H	2B	3B	HR	RBI	SB	BB	SO	AVG
1978	Helena (Pioneer)	56	190	34	59	6	6	1	23	15	26	42	.311
1979	Spartan (W. Caro.)	138	539	83	133	21	7	4	47	21	64	95	.247
1980	Reading (Eastern)	129	490	95	152	21	12	11	79	32	73	72	.310
1981	Okla. City (AA)	133	519	78	152	17	5	9	62	32	48	94	.293
1981	Philadelphia (NL)	13	6	2	1	0	0	0	0	0	0	1	.167
1982	Chicago (NL)	156	635	103	172	33	5	7	54	32	36	90	.271
1983	Chicago (NL)	158	633	94	165	25	4	8	48	37	51	79	.261
1984	Chicago (NL)	156	636	114	200	36	19	19	84	32	52	101	.314
1985	Chicago (NL)	153	609	113	186	31	6	26	83	54	57	97	.305
1986	Chicago (NL)	154	627	68	178	28	5	14	76	34	46	79	.284
1987	Chicago (NL)	132	523	81	154	25	2	16	59	21	59	79	.294
1988	Chicago (NL)	155	618	77	163	23	8	19	69	25	54	91	.264
1989	Chicago (NL)	157	606	104	176	25	5	30	76	15	59	85	.290
1990	Chicago (NL)	155	615	116	188	30	3	40	100	25	50	84	.306
1991	Chicago (NL)	158	585	104	170	32	2	26	100	22	87	89	.291
1992	Chicago (NL)	158	612	100	186	32	8	26	87	17	68	73	.304
1993	Chicago (NL)	117	456	67	141	20	0	9	45	9	37	62	.309
	MAJOR LEAGUE TOTALS	1822	7161	1143	2080	340	67	240	881	323	656	1010	.290

NATIONAL LEAGUE CHAMPIONSHIP SERIES RECORD

YEAR	TEAM (LEAGUE)	G	AB	R	H	2B	3B	HR	RBI	SB	BB	SO	AVG
1984	Chicago (NL)	5	19	3	7	2	0	0	2	3	3	2	.368
1989	Chicago (NL)	5	20	6	8	3	1	1	4	0	3	4	.400
	TOTALS	10	39	9	15	5	1	1	6	3	6	6	.385

ALL-STAR GAME RECORD

YEAR	LEAGUE	AB	R	H	2B	3B	HR	RBI	SB	BB	SO	AVG
1984	National	4	0	1	0	0	0	0	1	0	0	.250
1985	National	1	1	0	0	0	0	0	0	1	0	.000
1986	National	3	0	0	0	0	0	0	0	0	0	.000
1987	National	2	0	0	0	0	0	0	0	0	0	.000
1988	National	4	0	1	0	0	0	0	0	0	2	.250
1989	National	3	0	0	0	0	0	0	0	0	2	.000
1990	National	3	0	0	0	0	0	0	0	0	0	.000
1991	National	3	0	1	1	0	0	0	0	0	0	.333
1992	National	2	0	0	0	0	0	0	0	0	1	.000
1993	National	1	0	0	0	0	0	0	0	1	0	.000
	TOTALS	26	1	3	1	0	0	0	1	2	5	.115